THE **7** CONTINENTS

EUROPE

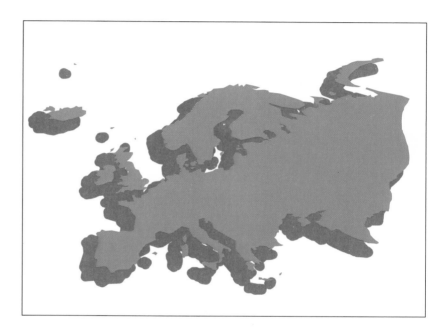

APRIL PULLEY SAYRE

TWENTY-FIRST CENTURY BOOKS
BROOKFIELD, CONNECTICUT

For "Andreandonni" our Italian friend(s).

—A.P.S.

Published by Twenty-First Century Books
A Division of The Millbrook Press, Inc.
2 Old New Milford Road
Brookfield, Connecticut 06804

Text copyright © 1998 by April Pulley Sayre
Maps by Joe LeMonnier
All rights reserved.

Library of Congress Cataloging-in-Publication Data
Sayre, April Pulley.
Europe / April Pulley Sayre.
p. cm. — (The Seven Continents)
Includes bibliographical references and index.
Summary: Describes unique characteristics of the European continent including
its landscapes, geology, weather and climate, rivers, coastlines, ocean air, and
soils as well as its plants, animals, and people.
ISBN 0-7613-3008-9
1. Europe—Juvenile literature. [1. Europe.] I. Title.
II. Series: Sayre, April Pulley. Seven Continents.
D907.S28 1998
940—dc21   97-35271
                                                        CIP
                                                        AC

Printed in the United States of America
5 4 3 2 1

Photo Credits

Cover photograph courtesy of M. Schneiders/H. Armstrong Roberts.

Photographs courtesy of Tony Stone Images: pp. 8 (© Erica Lansner), 12 (© John Freeman), 18 (© Phil Jason), 26 (© Hans Strand), 33 (© Arnulf Husmo), 36 (© Mittet Foto), 46 (© Tony Craddock); Gamma Liaison: pp. 10 (© Dean Berry), 39 (© Paul Souders), 42 (© Christian Vioujard), 49 (© Bill Swersey), 54 (© Didier Lebrun); Minden Pictures: p. 14 (© Frans Lanting); Animals Animals: pp. 15 (© J. Eastcott/Y. Momatiuk), 16 (© E. R. Degginger), 41 (left © Robert Maier), 53 (© Breck P. Kent); Woodfin Camp: pp. 21 (© J. Eastcott/ Y. Momatiuk), 57 (© Valdes/Lehtikuva); Uniphoto: p. 22 (© Nick Gheissari); Peter Arnold, Inc.: pp. 28 (© Jan-Peter Lahall), 41 (right © Gerard Lacz), 45 (© Otto Hahn).

CONTENTS

CONTINENTS: WHERE WE STAND

The ground you stand on may seem solid and stable, but it's really moving all the time. How is that possible? Because all of the earth's continents, islands, oceans, and people ride on tectonic plates. These plates, which are huge slabs of the earth's crust, float on top of hot, melted rock below. One plate may carry a whole continent and a piece of an ocean. Another may carry only a few islands and some ocean. The plates shift, slide, and even bump together slowly as the molten rock below them flows.

Plate edges are where the action is, geologically speaking. That's where volcanoes erupt and earthquakes shake the land. Tectonic plates collide, gradually crumpling continents into folds that become mountains. Dry land, or ocean floor, can be made at these plate edges. Melted rock, spurting out of volcanoes or oozing out of cracks between plates, cools and solidifies. Dry land, or ocean floor, can also be destroyed here, as the edge of one tectonic plate slips underneath another. The moving, grinding plates create tremendous pressure and heat, which melts the rock, turning it into semisolid material.

Continents, the world's largest landmasses, the rock rafts where we live, ride on this shifting puzzle of tectonic plates. These continents are made of material that floated to the surface when much of the earth was hot and liquid long ago. The floating material then cooled and became solid. Two hundred fifty million years ago, there was only one continent, the supercontinent Pangaea, surrounded by one ocean, Panthalassa. But since then, the tectonic plates have moved, breaking apart the continents and rearranging them. Today there are seven continents: North America, South America, Europe, Asia, Africa, Australia, and Antarctica.

250 Million Years Ago

Two hundred and fifty million years ago there was only one continent and one ocean, as shown above. (Rough shapes the continents would eventually take are outlined in black.) The view below shows where the seven continents are today. These positions will continue to change slowly as tectonic plates shift.

Present Day

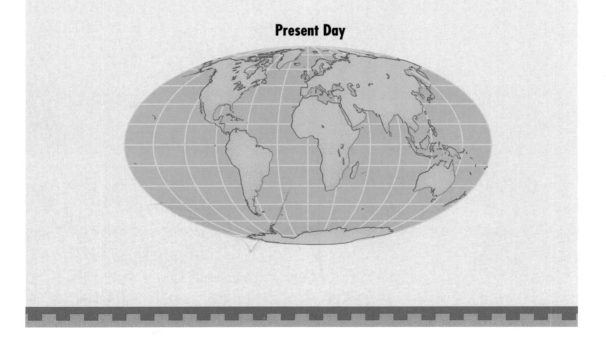

Each continent has its own unique character and conditions, shaped by its history and position on the earth. Europe, which is connected to Asia, has lots of coastline and moist, ocean air. Australia, meanwhile, is influenced by its neighbor, Antarctica, which sends cool currents northward to its shores. North America and South America were once separated, but are now connected by Panama. Over the years, animals, from ancient camels to armadillos, have traveled the bridge in between these two continents.

A continent's landscape, geology, weather, and natural communities affect almost every human action taken on that continent, from planting a seed to waging a war. Rivers become the borders of countries. Soil determines what we can grow. Weather and climate affect our cultures—what we feel, how we dress, even how we celebrate.

Understanding continents can give us a deeper knowledge of the earth—its plants, animals, and people. It can help us see behind news headlines to appreciate the forces that shape world events. Such knowledge can be helpful, especially in a world that's constantly changing and shifting, down to the very earth beneath our feet.

Russia, the largest country in the world, straddles the border between Europe and Asia. Pedestrians shown here are in St. Petersburg, in European Russia.

ONE

Keys to the Continent

Europe is known more for its cultural features than for its wildlife or physical geography. Tourists visiting Europe flock to see castles, cathedrals, museums, and mansions and to learn about its languages and cultures. But underneath the civilizations that created these attractions is a continent, complete with rivers, rainfall, soils, sunshine, flowers, and fungi. Europe has sunny meadows, vast green forests, and snow-capped mountains. It even has wild cats and wolves!

To get to know Europe, it's best to start from the ground up. Europe is the earth's second smallest continent. Only Australia is smaller. Yet the European continent does stretch from the cold arctic regions of Norway to the sunny southern tip of Spain. There it almost touches Africa; only 9.5 miles (15 kilometers) of sea lie in between.

The continent covers 4 million square miles (almost 11 million square kilometers) of the earth's surface, in all. To the west, the continent includes offshore islands such as Great Britain, Ireland, and the Faroes. Even Iceland, far to the west, is considered part of Europe! The reason these islands are considered part of the continent is that only shallow seas separate them from the mainland. The islands sit on the shelf of the continent, which is hidden beneath ocean water. Beyond the continental shelf, the ocean floor slopes steeply and the ocean is much deeper. (Islands that rise out of this deep ocean are considered oceanic islands and are not part of any continent.)

The eastern boundary between Europe and Asia is harder to pinpoint. In fact, some people consider Europe and Asia to be one continent, Eurasia. Others prefer to consider Europe separately, mainly for cultural reasons.

Much of Europe is rich agricultural land. Sunflowers fill the foreground of this photograph taken in Germany, while other crops can be seen in the background, growing on the hill below the castle.

For those who do consider Europe a continent, the eastern border begins at the Ural Mountains that cut across Russia from north to south. From the Urals, the dividing line between Europe and Asia runs down to the north shore of the Caspian Sea, then cuts westward along the crest of the Caucasus Mountains. The border skirts the north shore of the Black Sea and cuts off just a little chunk of Turkey, at the Bosporus strait, where the Black Sea connects with the Aegean Sea. The countries of Russia, Turkey, Kazakhstan, Georgia, and Azerbaijan straddle the traditional border and are shared by Europe and Asia. (Although geographers sometimes disagree about which countries should be considered part of Europe.)

Europe doesn't have the world's highest mountains or deepest canyons or biggest expanses of wilderness. But it does have many different biomes—living communities, such as arctic tundra, alpine tundra, taiga, temperate deciduous forest, and semidesert. Good weather, rich soil for growing crops, and productive fishing offshore and in their rivers and lakes, has helped European civilizations thrive.

CONTINENTAL INFLUENCES

- No part of Europe is very far from a coastline. And it has plenty of rivers. So Europe's people and products are transported easily by ship. For centuries, sailing ships—carrying explorers, merchants, and also armies—have helped spread European influence around the globe.
- Nearness to the Atlantic Ocean affects western Europe's weather. Warm ocean currents moderate the climate, making winters warm and summers cool.
- Europe is the only continent that has no hot desert. Much of the land is very fertile, and the weather is good for growing crops. These factors have allowed a dense population to settle on the continent.
- Europe does not hold world records for high mountains, large lakes, or other features. But the Caspian Sea it shares with Asia is the largest lake in the world.

STATISTICS AND RECORDS FOR THE CONTINENT OF EUROPE

- Area: 4,065,945 square miles (10,530,794 square kilometers)
- Population: 712,100,000
- Largest lake: Lake Ladoga, Russia, 6,835 square miles (17,703 square kilometers)
- Highest mountain: Mont Blanc, France, 15,771 feet (4,807 meters) tall
- Longest river: the Volga, which flows 2,194 miles (3,530 kilometers) across Russia and empties into the Caspian Sea
- Second longest river: the Danube, which flows 1,776 miles (2,858 kilometers) from Germany to the Black Sea

*The Giant's Causeway rises up like a staircase from the
sea on the coast of Antrim, Ireland.*

TWO

A TOUR OF NATURAL WONDERS

Most European guidebooks will direct you to palaces, restaurants, and museums. But there are other places to explore. Europe has a wilder side—places where natural wonders can be seen, experienced, and enjoyed.

A tour of "natural" Europe could begin in Iceland. Even in the middle of winter, you could take a hot dip in one of Reykjavik's volcanically heated pools. You can be toasty warm in steaming water, while snow is on the ground all around. In the city of Reykjavik and elsewhere in Iceland, it's common to swim outdoors in naturally heated pools. Groundwater—water underground—flows through rocks heated by volcanic activity; that's why it's hot when it surfaces.

There are other natural European features you might want to visit:

• On northern Ireland's coast, you could take a walk on Giant's Causeway, a strange rock formation that has mystified people for years. The Causeway is made of tremendous stone columns, each about 18 inches (46 centimeters) in diameter and as much as 600 feet (180 meters) high. Pillars of different heights make this coastal region look like a staircase for giants climbing onto shore. The "stairs" were made long ago by molten rock emerging from inside the earth, cooling quickly, becoming solid, then cracking in crystal shapes.

• Peek over Bempton Cliffs, in England. But don't get too near the edge! The drop is 400 feet (122 meters) down to jagged rocks and crashing waves below. On Bempton Cliffs you can see and hear noisy seabirds swirling in the air. Bempton has the largest

Lynx have tufts of hair on their ears and large feet that work like snowshoes in winter weather.

colony of seabirds on Great Britain's mainland. Tens of thousands of puffins, gannets, kittiwakes, fulmars, and guillemots nest on the chalk cliffs' edges, ledges, and crevices.

• Be sure to visit the fabulous fjords of Norway, which have some of the most dramatic scenery on earth. The fjords began long ago as huge valleys carved by glaciers—rivers of ice that pushed across the land. When the glaciers melted, the sea level rose and flooded these valleys, and they became fjords. On a boat, you can sail up into a fjord, where dramatic cliffs, full of nesting seabirds, rise on either side. Snow-capped peaks tower above. In some places glaciers, left over from the last Ice Age (about 30,000 years ago) are still visible at the fjord's end.

• Trek through Sweden's national parks, such as Sarek and Abisko. You'll see glaciers and mountain peaks. In Sweden's wild forests, if you're very lucky, you might catch sight of a lynx, a type of wildcat. You can also hike, camp, and pick berries almost anywhere in the countryside because of a national tradition called *allemansrätten. Allemansrätten,* which means right of public access, allows people to camp on and walk across private lands as long as they respect nature and other people's privacy.

• Visit Lake Balaton in Hungary and try fishing. This 230-square-mile (600-square-kilometer) lake is the largest in central Europe. But watch out for the sudden, violent thunderstorms that brew over the lake in summer. They could really rock your boat!

• Take a steamer trip down Europe's longest river, the Volga, as it passes by Russian farms, villages, and industrial plants. You'll see why this river, called *matushka,* or "little mother," by the Russians, is the heart of the country's agriculture and industry.

Freedom Cave is one example of the outstanding rock formations found in caves in the border region between Slovakia and Hungary.

• Take a stroll on Lithuania's Baltic beaches. The Baltic isn't as salty as most seas, because so many rivers flow into it and its connection to the ocean is small. On Baltic beaches you may find pebbles of amber—honey-colored fossilized tree sap. Insects from millions of years ago are sometimes preserved inside the sap!

• Explore Bialowieza National Park in Poland, where ancient trees grow and European forest bison roam. Bialowieza's forest has been protected since the fifteenth century, originally as hunting grounds for royalty. Today it contains elk, boar, wolves, lynx, otters, beavers, and some of the best undisturbed forest in Europe.

• Bring a flashlight to explore the spectacular caves and caverns on the border of Slovakia and Hungary. Stalactites and stalagmites, and bats, wolves, boars, and wildcats can be found in the region preserved by Hungary's Aggtelek National Park and Slovakia's Slovensky Kras Protected Area.

The waters off Greece are perfect for all sorts of water sports.
This is a view of the harbor at Mykonos, Greece.

• Autumn is a good time to explore Europe's largest canyon, which runs through Yugoslavia's Djerdap National Park and Romania's Cazanele Forest Reserve. The canyon's oak-beech-walnut forests turn red and gold, and the views are breathtaking.

• Greece, with warm waters, good winds, and more than two thousand islands, is an excellent place to try windsurfing or other kinds of sailing. You might even sail past ancient ruins, straight out of history. Just wear plenty of sunscreen because in southern Europe the sun can be very intense.

• In northwestern Slovenia, go white-water rafting on the beautiful Soca River, which runs out of the Alps, a chain of mountains that curve through Switzerland, Austria, Italy, and France. Once you're done, try hiking. Or, wait until winter and try skiing, which is wildly popular among Slovenia's residents.

• In summer, you could hike through meadows of colorful wildflowers in the Alps. If you're a risk-taker, you might climb the Matterhorn, a peak in the Swiss Alps. The Matterhorn's steep sides were once considered unclimbable. But since it was first scaled in 1865, this 14,691-foot (4,478-meter) mountain has been climbed by thousands of people. Yet even now the climb is perilous. Each year many people die trying to conquer this challenging peak.

• Legend has it that Romulus and Remus, the founders of Rome, were raised by a mother wolf. These days, real wolves can be found not far from Rome, hiding in small stands of trees. These wolves are gray wolves, the same species as the ones found in Alaska, Canada, and Minnesota. But you'll have to look hard to find wolves—they're very secretive. Only about five hundred live in Italy. The wolves feed on deer, wild boars, small animals, garbage, and—to the dismay of the locals—sheep from nearby herds.

• Definitely bring your binoculars if you visit Cévennes National Park, in France. You might see a vulture soaring over the granite mountains and forests of pine, chestnut, fir, and oak. Bring a raincoat, too, if you plan to hike Mount Aigoual, whose name means "watery mountain." It's the wettest place in France, receiving 89 inches (226 centimeters) of rain per year!

• Stop by Coto Doñana, Spain's largest park. Many birds do. They rest and feed at Coto Doñana's mudflats, marshes, dunes, and shrub lands to fuel up after crossing the Mediterranean Sea from Africa. Eagles, flamingos, herons, egrets, and spoonbills can all be seen in the park.

These are just a few of the many natural wonders you can seek out in Europe. But some of the best wild encounters you'll have may be the ones you simply stumble across: a fog creeping in over a Russian bog, icicles hanging on an Austrian cliff, or a whale spouting off Norway's coast. These sights are not only enjoyable; they hint at the natural features that shape Europeans' lives.

This satellite image taken at night shows Europe, a land of peninsulas.
The illuminated areas are cities.

THREE

THE LAY OF THE LAND

In many ways, Europe is a water continent. Look at a map and you'll see why. Europe's coastline is jagged, crooked, and wavy, with lots of peninsulas—portions of land that jut out into the ocean or a sea. (In fact, some geographers consider Europe to be merely a peninsula of the continent of Asia!) No region of Europe is very far from a coastline. That's very different from most other continents. Africa, Asia, and North America, for instance, have vast central plains that are nowhere near a coastline.

Europe's many peninsulas and inlets provide great places for seaports, where fishing boats, cargo ships, and ocean liners find safe harbors. Europe also has plenty of rivers, which form even more routes for shipping goods out to sea. It's no wonder Europeans have developed into world-famous explorers, fishers, sailors, and merchants. For centuries they've traveled the oceans to seek new lands, fish, spices, silks, and other goods. Living on a continent with easy access to the ocean has shaped Europeans' way of life. Other natural features such as mountain ranges, volcanoes, and low plains have affected their lives, too.

LOOKING HIGH AND LOW

From high, snow-capped mountains in Italy to soggy lowlands beneath sea level in the Netherlands, Europe has all kinds of highs and lows. The continent's assortment of landforms—mountains, valleys, plateaus, plains, and peninsulas—give its landscape variety.

19

AWESOME ALPS AND MORE

Europe has five major mountain ranges: the Alps, the Pyrenees, the Caucasus, the Carpathians, and the Urals. The Alps, which run through France, Switzerland, Austria, and Italy, have magnificent snow-capped peaks; some reach more than 10,000 feet (3,050 meters) above sea level. The Pyrenees divide Spain from France. The Carpathian Mountains form a crescent from Slovakia and Poland, through the Ukraine, and into Romania. The Caucasus Mountains run between the Black Sea and the Caspian Sea. And the ancient, worn-down Ural Mountains in Russia mark the border between Europe and Asia.

WHICH IS THE HIGHEST?

In Europe, the top of the highest mountain is not the highest point on the continent. How is this possible? Because the methods for measuring the highest mountain and the highest point are different. Europe's highest mountain, nestled in the French Alps, is Mont Blanc, which towers 15,771 feet (4,807 meters) tall. That distance is measured from the mountain's base to the mountain's top. In contrast, the highest point in Europe is measured starting from sea level. So, Mount Elbrus, which sits on land already high above sea level, has a "head start," measurement wise. Even though it's not as tall as Mont Blanc, Mount Elbrus, in Russia, tops out at 18,510 feet (5,642 meters) above sea level. That makes it the highest point in Europe.

HILLY PLATEAUS

North of the Alps is a region of immense plateaus called the central uplands. Like tables, plateaus are elevated areas that are relatively flat on top. (Mountains are pointy and jagged, instead.) Europe's plateaus, located in southern Germany, northern Austria, southeastern France, and the Czech Republic, have gentle hills through which Europe's famous Danube and Rhine Rivers flow. Factories, which use river water in their production processes and to transport products by boat, are found along the rivers. Castles, too, perch on crags above the rivers. (The fortresses once held armies that fought off invaders traveling by ship.) Cool, wet weather supports green grass, where beef cattle, dairy cattle, and sheep graze.

THE NORTHERN EUROPEAN PLAIN

In geography, *plain* doesn't mean something that's simple or not fancy. A plain is a landform: a flat expanse of land. The Northern European Plain begins at the Pyrenees Mountains, which separate Spain from France, curves around France and across northern Europe, then widens toward the Ural Mountains in Russia. This plain has a gently rolling landscape and rich soils. Light rains fall year-round, so the region is excellent for growing crops, such as corn, barley, wheat, and potatoes.

Crops in the field form a patchwork background behind a
Polish farmer and his plowhorse.

Rivers, including the Dnieper, Volga, and Rhine, run through the plain, making it suitable for human settlements and industry. Major cities—Paris, Berlin, Minsk, and Moscow—thrive in the abundance of resources here. But centuries ago, this broad, flat area in Russia and the Ukraine was a path for conquerors—the Huns and Mongols, who pushed into Europe from Asia. No mountains stood in their way. Even in the last two world wars, Poland, whose name means "plain," has been vulnerable to invasion because it does not have any mountainous borders to protect it from invading armies.

HOLDING BACK THE SEA

Who lives below the sea? Many people in the Netherlands. They're not actually underwater. But they do farm and even live below sea level. Motors constantly pump ocean water out, to keep it from flooding the land. This land was once coastal marsh and shallow ocean bottom near shore. Then, people drained it and turned it into farmland and towns. This process is called "reclamation." For almost a thousand years, the people of

Canals serve as waterways in Amsterdam and elsewhere in the Netherlands.

the Netherlands have reclaimed land, at one time using windmills to power the water pumps. Dikes, which are artificial ditches, hold and channel coastal rivers and ocean water, keeping it out of the fields and yards. Today, two-fifths of the Netherlands is made of reclaimed land.

RUGGED REGIONS

In contrast to the green, fertile plain of Europe are the rugged highlands. These geologically old, worn-down mountains have rocky, thin soil. (Some rocks here are more than a billion years old!) Growing crops is difficult, so grazing sheep and goats is common. Very few people settle on the land. Rugged highlands exist in Scandinavia —the region that includes Norway, Sweden, and Denmark. Parts of the United Kingdom, France, Spain, and Portugal also have such rugged regions.

PLACE OF PENINSULAS

Europe is made of many peninsulas. The Scandinavian Peninsula contains Norway and Sweden. Another peninsula, Denmark, juts out from northern Europe. The boot-shaped peninsula of Italy seems about to kick the island of Sicily across the Mediterranean Sea. To the southeast, the Balkan Peninsula stretches from Italy toward Turkey and the Aegean Sea. The Iberian Peninsula, the squarish piece of land made up of Portugal, Spain, and Gibraltar is divided from the rest of Europe by the Pyrenees Mountains.

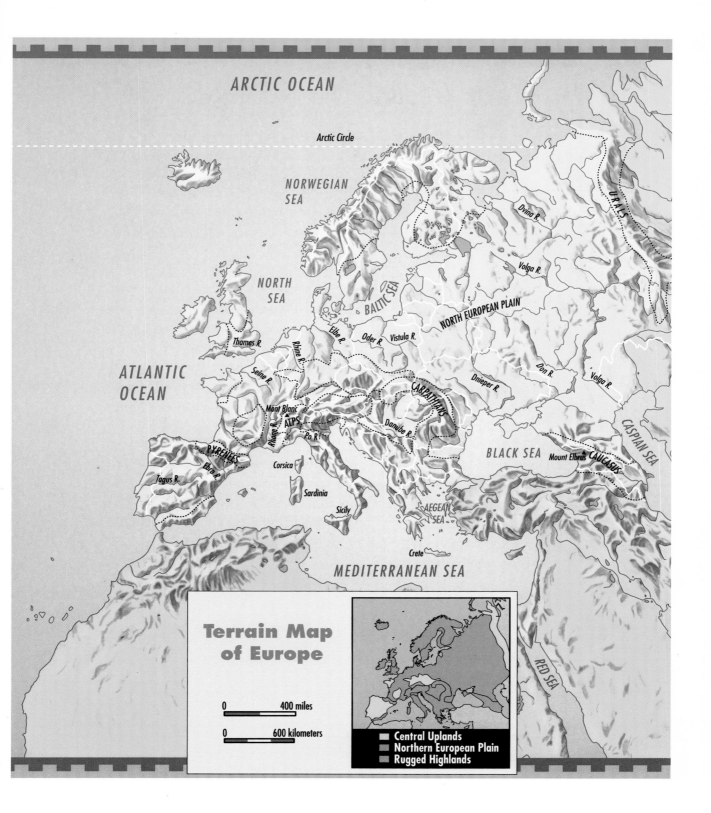

ARCTIC OCEAN

Arctic Circle

NORWEGIAN
SEA

NORTH
SEA

ATLANTIC
OCEAN

BALTIC SEA

NORTH EUROPEAN PLAIN

Dvina R.

Volga R.

URALS

Thames R.

Seine R.

Rhine R.

Elbe R.

Oder R.

Vistula R.

Dnieper R.

Don R.

Volga R.

Mont Blanc

ALPS

Rhone R.

Po R.

CARPATHIANS

Danube R.

BLACK SEA

Mount Elbrus

CAUCASUS

CASPIAN SEA

PYRENEES

Ebro R.

Corsica

Tagus R.

Sardinia

Sicily

AEGEAN
SEA

Crete

MEDITERRANEAN SEA

RED SEA

Terrain Map of Europe

0	400 miles
0	600 kilometers

Central Uplands
Northern European Plain
Rugged Highlands

Don't Forget the Water

Without water, Europe's landscape just wouldn't be the same. Four great river systems dominate the continent: the Rhine, the Danube, the Dnieper, and the Volga. The Rhine and the Danube spring up in the Alps. The Rhine then flows northward through Germany and the Netherlands and empties into the North Sea. The Danube winds eastward through Austria, Hungary, and Romania, eventually pouring into the Black Sea. The Dnieper drains the famous Pripet marshes of southwestern Belarus and flows through the Ukraine into the Black Sea. The Volga flows south through Russia into the Caspian Sea at the port of Astrakhan, where gigantic pink lotus blossoms bloom. Other major European rivers include the Don, the Dvina, the Ebro, the Elbe, the Oder, the Po, the Rhone, the Seine, the Tagus, the Thames, the Ural, and the Vistula.

Rivers Tie It All Together

For thousands of years, rivers have been the lifeblood of Europe. Flooding rivers have brought fertile mud to farms along riverbanks. Farmers have taken their vegetables, wool, and meat to market by boat and by raft. Many major cities in Europe are located along rivers. In Medieval times, Berlin, Germany, was built near the junction of two rivers because transporting goods to and from other towns was easy by boat. And in the Carpathian Mountains, the "Iron Gate," a gorge carved out by the Danube, was a route for explorers, merchants, and armies for centuries.

Today, the impact of European rivers can still be seen. The Rhine is a watery highway, western Europe's most important route for transporting farm goods and industrial products. Where rivers do not run, many canals and waterways have been built in order to link rivers, the ocean, and commercial shipping sites. Even the energy of many rivers, such as the Rhone, which runs through Switzerland and France, has been harnessed by hydroelectric dams, which provide electricity.

Don't Believe What You "Sea"

Between Europe and Asia are two tremendous bodies of water—the Black Sea and the Caspian Sea. The Caspian Sea is so big, it's almost the size of Sweden. It is the world's largest inland sea. The Black Sea is bigger than Japan. The Black Sea isn't really black in color; its name probably came from the dark clouds and violent storms that arise frequently in winter over its waters. Though plagued by pollution, the Black Sea isn't entirely inhospitable. In Romania, children swim in the Black Sea and tourists visit its shores. Where the Danube pours into the Black Sea is a tremendous wildlife sanctuary, full of forests, marshes, and streams where pelicans, egrets, ibises, herons, and hundreds of other bird species nest and feed. The Black Sea is connected to the Aegean Sea through a tiny opening called the Strait of Bosporus, near

Istanbul, Turkey. (The Caspian Sea, shared by Europe with Asia, will be covered in this series in the volume about Asia.)

EUROPE'S ICY SECRET

Europe is affected by water in more than just its liquid form. The continent's weather and landscape have also been shaped by ice. About 2.5 million years ago, the earth

---

SHAKE, RATTLE, AND ROLL

Usually it's hard to see the results of activity at tectonic seams because they're under the ocean. But in Iceland, tectonic plates meet on dry ground. Iceland sits on the seam between the North American and Eurasian plates. As a result, earthquakes frequently shake Iceland, and volcanic eruptions are common there. In 1963, an underwater eruption formed a new island: Surtsey.

Plate activity affects Europe elsewhere, too. For instance, the Alps are growing taller, by about an inch (2¹/₂ centimeters) a year. These young mountains started forming about 40 million years ago, when the African plate drifted northward, pushing into the Eurasian plate. The Pyrenees, Apennines, and Carpathians formed then, too, folding and pushing upward, under pressure. Meanwhile, Africa trapped part of the ocean, creating the Mediterranean Sea.

The rise of the Alps may not be very noticeable, but other activity along the plate edges is. Except in Iceland, most of Europe is far from these plate edges. However, southern Europe, in the Mediterranean, lies at a plate edge—in a major volcano and earthquake zone. If you really want to see what the power of nature can do, visit the ruins of Pompeii, in Italy. Pompeii was a city buried under ash and mud from the eruption of Mount Vesuvius in A.D. 79. Geologic activity has continued to occur in southern Europe. In 1963, a 6.0 magnitude earthquake destroyed most of Skopje, Yugoslavia, which is now in Macedonia. In 1980, a 7.2 magnitude earthquake hit southern Italy, killing thousands of people. On September 26, 1997, a 5.6 magnitude earthquake hit Foligno, Italy, killing several people, destroying homes, and damaging the famous Basilica of St. Francis of Assisi, in the town of Assisi.

Mediterranean Europe is a major earthquake zone because underneath it, the African and Eurasian tectonic plates grind together. The intense pressure at the plate edges melts rock, and volcanoes form. In Italy, people have settled on the slopes of Mounts Vesuvius and Etna, despite knowing that these volcanoes could erupt again at any time. The slopes are fertile, thus good for growing crops, and they are home to many people who find it hard to leave this beautiful region.

25

*Sunrise casts a glow over Iceland's Vatnajökull Glacier
and icebergs floating nearby.*

cooled, and ice sheets developed over much of Europe. This was the beginning of the Ice Age. Since that time, the earth's climate—its long-term weather patterns and trends—has been cool at times and warm at others. (In France, there are thirty-thousand-year-old cave paintings that show hyenas and rhinoceroses—evidence that these creatures lived in Europe during warmer times.)

During the Ice Age, the weather was cold, and much of the earth's water froze into ice. Glaciers—gigantic rivers of ice as much as a mile thick—covered much of the land. With so much water tied up as ice, there was less liquid water available. So ocean levels were lower, and more land was exposed. That's why, during the Ice Age, you could have walked from Britain to France. So much water was frozen into ice that there wasn't any ocean separating the British Isles and the European mainland!

Right now, the earth's climate is fairly warm. Most of the glaciers have melted. Yet glaciers still exist; they're just much smaller than during the various ice ages. Europe's biggest glacier, Vatnajökull, lies in Iceland. The glacier's ice is 3,000 feet (900 meters) thick!

Europe's icy history is written in stone. During ice ages, glaciers, like tremendous bulldozers, made their mark on the land. Glaciers scraped valleys, called glens, into Scotland's landscape. In Norway, glaciers carved valleys that later filled in with seawater and became fjords. All over northern Europe you can still find rocks with scratch marks left by glaciers thousands of years ago as they pushed ice, rock, and soil over the continent. These marks remind Europeans of their continent's icy past.

Ice covers a lake in Sweden. Snow can be seen on the mountains beyond in a photograph taken in the month of June.

FOUR

THE INFLUENCE OF THE OCEAN

If you had to pack a suitcase for a trip throughout Europe, you'd need an awfully big bag. You'd want bathing suits and light clothes for lounging on hot, sunny Greek islands. You'd need a raincoat for London's rain and fog. And in winter, visiting northern Russia, you'd want a parka, a sweater, a hat, and long underwear to beat the chill of icy arctic winds.

Europe's weather varies day to day, season to season, and place to place. Its climate has even changed over the millennia. Thirty thousand years ago, during the last ice age, the Netherlands was a cold, forbidding place, smothered in ice more than 1,000 feet (300 meters) thick. Back then, growing flowers there might have seemed laughable. Yet tulip farms blanket large parts of the Netherlands today.

Despite long-term changes, Europe's weather and climate do show general patterns. Sweden is cool. Iceland is windy. Greece is hot and dry in summer, cooler and wetter in winter. Knowing these kinds of patterns can help you understand all sorts of things, from where plants and animals live to why there are more outdoor cafés in Italy than in Iceland!

WEATHER AND CLIMATE SHAPERS

Most people know that the countries near the North or South Poles are very cold and that countries near the equator are warm. So it's not surprising that a country's weather and climate are affected by its latitude (its position in terms of distance from the equator). Because of the earth's position in space, countries near the poles receive only slanted rays from the sun. But the sun shines directly on countries near the equator, which is why they get more sunlight per square inch of land and heat up faster than those near the poles.

Like most of the eastern United States, mainland Europe has a relatively mild climate. As a result, many people imagine that Europe is just across the ocean from the United States, at about the same latitude. The big surprise is that Europe is, in fact, much farther north, at a higher latitude. Parts of Sweden, Finland, and Norway are north of the Arctic Circle. Most of Europe is at about the same latitude as Labrador, far up in Canada. If a New Yorker could look eastward, across the ocean, they'd see not France or Britain, but sunny Portugal instead!

WARM CURRENTS

The reason western Europe has a milder climate than North American cities at the same latitude is that winds blowing over warm ocean currents warm it up. The Gulf Stream, a powerful current, brings warm water north from the equator. This warm water helps keep many European ports free of ice even in winter. Wind blowing from the west to the east also pushes warm air, which is heated by the warm water, over the land.

MARINE MODERATOR

The ocean moderates Europe's climate in other ways. That's because liquid water can slowly absorb or release a tremendous amount of heat. (It takes more energy to heat up water than it does to heat up air.) As a result, an ocean, sea, bay, or lake may remain warmer in the fall and cooler in the spring than the surrounding land. These bodies of water absorb or release heat slowly, so temperatures over nearby lands don't rise or fall very quickly. The Atlantic Ocean, the Mediterranean Sea, and lakes within Europe all have this effect on the land nearby.

SOGGY BUT STABLE

Another feature that regulates western European climate is humidity. Humidity (the amount of water vapor in the air) has a moderating effect on temperatures. The level of humidity determines how quickly air warms up or cools off. For instance, dry desert air heats up quickly in the sun and loses heat quickly when the sun sets. Humid air, on the other hand, heats up and cools off more slowly. Western Europe has relatively humid air, so there are fewer extremes of temperature there than in dry climates.

LOOK HOW HIGH: ALTITUDE'S EFFECTS

More than latitude, wind currents, and nearness to the ocean influence weather. Altitude—how high above sea level a place is—also changes weather drastically. People can sit on warm beaches at the base of a mountain, while skiers slide down snow-packed slopes above. In Europe, as elsewhere, altitude makes a difference, especially in the Alps.

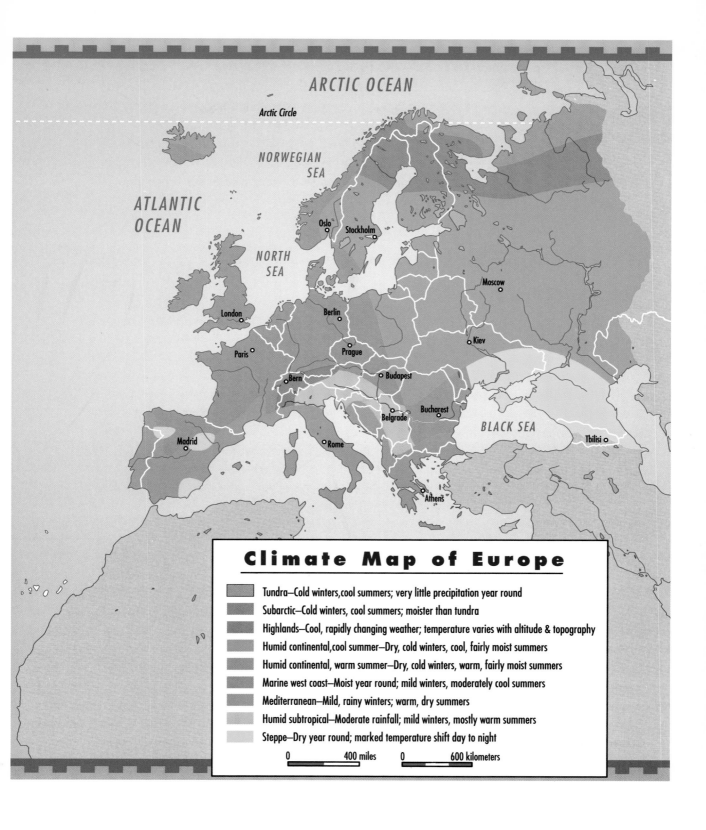

ARCTIC OCEAN

Arctic Circle

NORWEGIAN SEA

ATLANTIC OCEAN

NORTH SEA

Oslo

Stockholm

Moscow

London

Berlin

Kiev

Paris

Prague

Bern

Budapest

Bucharest

Belgrade

BLACK SEA

Tbilisi

Madrid

Rome

Athens

Climate Map of Europe

Tundra—Cold winters, cool summers; very little precipitation year round

Subarctic—Cold winters, cool summers; moister than tundra

Highlands—Cool, rapidly changing weather; temperature varies with altitude & topography

Humid continental, cool summer—Dry, cold winters, cool, fairly moist summers

Humid continental, warm summer—Dry, cold winters, warm, fairly moist summers

Marine west coast—Moist year round; mild winters, moderately cool summers

Mediterranean—Mild, rainy winters; warm, dry summers

Humid subtropical—Moderate rainfall; mild winters, mostly warm summers

Steppe—Dry year round; marked temperature shift day to night

0   400 miles   0   600 kilometers

ALL BECAUSE OF POTATOES

A hundred and fifty years ago, more than a million people in Ireland died—all for the lack of potatoes. Over the course of several years, fields of potatoes in Ireland, and elsewhere in Europe, died because of potato blight, a fungus that rots the leaves, stems, and tubers of potato plants.

The reason the Irish were so dependent on potatoes has to do with both climate and history. In the mid-1500s, explorers brought potatoes to Europe from South America. In the humid, temperate climate of Ireland, growing grains such as wheat and barley had always been a risky business, with many crop failures. The weather was often too wet or too cool. But potatoes grew well and were easy to store, so they soon became a popular crop.

During winter in Ireland, many people ate only potatoes. So when the potato crops failed in those winters from 1845 to 1852, people went hungry. Weakened by hunger, many died of disease. One out of every eight people in Ireland died. It was a horrible time: a time the Irish called *An Gorta Mor,* the Great Hunger.

Unlike South American farmers, the Irish farmers grew relatively few kinds of potatoes, and all of these were affected by the blight in the mid-1800s. Not only did a million Irish people die during the potato famine, but more than a million and a half emigrated, many to North America. In just a few years, a fungus and the potato had drastically changed both Irish and American history.

THE BIG PICTURE: CLIMATIC REGIONS

According to scientists, Europe has nine different kinds of climate. But three main climate types are dominant: marine west coast, humid continental, and Mediterranean.

EUROPE'S NINE CLIMATE TYPES

Marine West Coast, Humid Subtropical, Mediterranean, Steppe, Humid Continental with warm summer, Humid Continental with cool summer, Subarctic, Tundra, Highland (Mountain)

MARINE WEST COAST CLIMATE

Western Europe, from the British Isles to northern Spain to western Poland, experiences a mild climate called marine west coast climate. This climate is generally damp, with few temperature extremes. It's similar to the climate of the eastern United States. The ocean moderates the climate, preventing swings in temperature.

HUMID CONTINENTAL CLIMATE

Continental climate is always found in a continent's interior, relatively far from the ocean. In Europe, the region of continental climate stretches from Sweden, Poland, and Romania, through Russia and into Asia. Lacking the moderating effects of the ocean, these places can experience temperature extremes. Asia's Gobi desert, for instance, can get very hot or very cold. Europe's continental climate is slightly different; it's more humid. So it doesn't experience quite the temperature extremes of the Gobi. Europe's continental climate tends to be very cold and snowy in the winter. Summers are relatively cool, although in a few southern regions, it can become quite warm.

MEDITERRANEAN CLIMATE

Southern Europe—Spain, Portugal, Italy, the south of France, and Greece—have a Mediterranean climate, meaning their winters are damp, but not very cold. Summers are warm and dry. This kind of climate is also found in South America, in Chile; in North America, in California; and in Africa, in South Africa. All of these places have similar weather, and some similar plants, too.

Europe's continental climate brings snowy winters to Oslo, Norway. Here, the Royal Palace is surrounded by snow-covered parkland.

When the *scirocco* blows, Italians know the weather will be sticky and hot. *Scirocco* is their name for the wind that carries hot air all the way from the Libyan deserts of North Africa onto their shores. This wind, as it crosses over the Mediterranean Sea, picks up moisture from the waters below. So when it arrives in Italy, the wind is both hot and moist. It's best to keep a handkerchief handy for wiping sweat off your brow when the *scirocco* is blowing. On better days along the Mediterranean, Italians welcome the *maestro,* not an orchestra conductor, but a less humid wind that brings sunny weather.

Spain has hot winds, too. In summer, the *leveche,* a hot, dry wind from North Africa, raises temperatures. Even worse is the *solano,* which brings heat, dust, and humidity to Spain's Mediterranean shores, making outdoor sports uncomfortable.

Elsewhere, warm winds can be disastrous. Skiers in the Swiss or Austrian Alps keep an eye out for a *föhn,* a warm dry wind. It melts snow, sometimes causing avalanches. When the *föhn* blows in, local temperatures can shoot up 30°F (17°C) in a single hour!

Cool winds also affect Europe's weather. When the *mistral* is coming, people in Marseilles, France, put on their warmest coats. That's because this southerly wind brings cold, dry air from farther north. In Hungary, the *bora,* another wind from the north or northeast, brings colder temperatures. But cold winds aren't always unpleasant. As they lounge on the beach, summer tourists in Romania and Bulgaria may welcome the cool afternoon breezes that blow in from the Black Sea.

WHEN ZERO MEANS IT'S FREEZING

If you are visiting Greece, and someone says it's going to be 32 degrees that day, don't put on a winter coat. You'll want summer clothing. That's because in Europe temperatures and other measurements are given in the International System of Units. Degrees Celsius are the unit of temperature measurement. In this system, 32 degrees Celsius is actually 89.6 degrees in Fahrenheit—toasty warm! The International System of Units is used just about everywhere in the world except the United States. The United States uses the English System of measurement, instead.

Celsius temperatures are based on a very sensible, easy-to-remember scale: 0°C is the freezing point of water and 100°C is the boiling point. Using Fahrenheit temperatures, in the English System, the freezing point of water is 32°F and the boiling point is 212°F.

MAKING CONNECTIONS: WIND, SOIL, AND ACID RAIN

Wind isn't just important to sailors. And soil isn't just a farmer's concern. These aspects of the environment affect forests, fish, and crops people depend upon—sometimes in surprising ways. One good example is how wind and soil interact with pollution, specifically, in the case of acid rain.

THE DEATH OF EUROPEAN FORESTS

In the early 1980s, Germans could see that their forests were dying. Trees' needles were turning yellow and falling off. The Germans called the phenomenon *waldsterben,* which means "forest death." Today, more than half of all the trees in Germany, Greece, Switzerland, Scandinavia, Great Britain, and the Netherlands, and more than three-quarters of the trees in Poland, Belarus, and Russia are damaged, dying, or dead.

Acid rain led to the forest die-offs. Chemicals called sulfates and other air pollutants from running cars, factories, and power plants mix with rain, snow, and moisture in the air, making them more acidic. This produces acid rain. Scientists believe that acid rain weakens trees, reducing their resistance to disease, cold winters, insect attacks, and other causes of tree death. Acid rain, as it washes through the soil, also releases natural minerals that can kill fish, frogs, and plants.

WIND, SOIL, AND ACID RAIN

What do wind and soil have to do with acid rain? Ask the people of Scandinavia. Acid rain damage in Norway and Sweden is particularly severe. Thousands of lakes there are now lifeless—the fish and frogs killed off by acid rain. Yet these countries produce relatively little air pollution. It turns out that 90 percent of the air pollution that affects Norway and Sweden blows in on the wind from other countries, especially those in eastern Europe. (That's one reason why Sweden is spending so much money to help eastern European countries install better pollution controls.)

Another reason Norway and Sweden are so severely damaged by acid rain is because their soil is naturally acidic. As a result, the soil does not neutralize very much of the acid that falls. Acid rain damage occurs more quickly than it does in other places that have less acidic soil that can offset the acid's effects. Acid rain is one more phenomenon that's easier to understand if you know a continent's weather, climate, and geology.

*In Norway, a Saami child in traditional dress leads
a reindeer away from a herd.*

FIVE

A BIRD'S-EYE VIEW OF BIOMES

If you were a bird, flying over the continent of Europe, you'd see a spectacular variety of scenes. To the north, you'd see vast, cold, treeless lands, where reindeer graze and arctic hares hop. Farther south, you'd fly over green forests of pointed trees, where lynx run and birds eat seeds from cones. Elsewhere, you could soar over grasslands, full of flowers, or skirt shrub lands that are dry and hot.

For a small continent, Europe has a wide variety of biomes—areas that have a certain kind of community of plants and animals. Europe's major terrestrial, or land, biomes include arctic tundra, taiga, temperate deciduous forest, temperate grassland, and the Mediterranean biome.

TUNDRA: TREELESS BUT TERRIFIC

If you lived in the far north, in Mermansk, Russia, for instance, you would be surrounded by arctic tundra. The arctic tundra covers much of Iceland, Norway, and the northern tips of Sweden, Finland, and Russia. Arctic tundra is cold, dry, and windy, with only low-growing plants. Frozen ground prevents trees from growing there. Conditions are so harsh that plants grow in low mounds, or trail across the ground, so they're out of the wind, and protected from the extremely cold air by the snow. Because the climate is cold much of the year, only the top layer of soil thaws in summer. That leaves a layer of frozen ground, called permafrost, that may reach hundreds of feet deep. In summer, you could dig a hole and store your food in the ground, which is always freezer-cold.

WINTER WHITES

In winter, birds called ptarmigans, ermines, and some arctic foxes shed their dark summer coats. They grow new white fur or feathers that acts as camouflage, making them less visible in the snow. White fur and feathers also contain pockets of air. This layer of air may help insulate white-coated animals from the cold. Dark fur and feathers contain pigment and do not insulate as well.

REAL REINDEER

Perhaps the most famous European tundra resident is the reindeer. Reindeer are the same species as the caribou of Alaska and Canada. Reindeer spend summer in the tundra and winter in the taiga. They feed on grasses, mosses, and lichen, which are plantlike partnerships of fungi and algae. Many reindeer are domestic animals, herded by native people called the Saami. (The Saami, who live in northern Scandinavia and northwestern Russia, were once known by outsiders as Laplanders.) Although many Saami still wear clothing made of reindeer hide and follow their traditional lifestyle, some also use modern machines, such as snowmobiles and helicopters, to herd reindeer.

THE CIRCUMPOLAR SCENE

Numerous tundra animals and plant species are circumpolar, meaning they live on islands and continents all around the pole. For instance, snowy owls, arctic hares, ermines, musk oxen, wolves, lemmings, arctic foxes, and wolverines can be found not only on European tundra but on North American tundra as well. Some of these animals may spread from continent to continent and island to island by walking across frozen ocean in winter or by riding on floating icebergs.

TAIGA: THE SPRUCE-MOOSE FOREST

Imagine a forest with mossy, spongy ground and tall, pointed trees like Christmas trees, only much larger. Imagine a woodpecker tapping on a tree, a moose munching on bog plants, or a brown bear eating blueberries. These are scenes you would see outside the town of Lycksele, Sweden, which is in the taiga biome. Taiga, a vast belt of forest, covers Sweden, Finland, and northern Russia. Taiga, which is also called boreal forest, or northern coniferous forest, occurs in Canada and parts of Alaska, as well.

CONE COUNTRY

Taiga is dominated by conifers: trees that bear their seeds in cones. There's even a resident bird called the crossbill, which has a crossed bill, perfect for prying seeds out of cones. Conifers have very narrow, wax-covered leaves, often called needles. Pine needles and spruce needles are examples. Most conifers are also evergreen—meaning they do not

*A sign warns of reindeer crossing the road in Norway.
The sign might be marked "Caribou Crossing" in Alaska and Canada!*

drop their leaves all at once, in fall. (One exception is larch, also called tamarack, a conifer species that *does* drop its needles in fall.) Taiga trees have shallow roots because they grow in the shallow soil layer above the permafrost. The soil is relatively poor for growing other kinds of plants, so there's little farming in the taiga.

SQUISHY SPOTS

In between patches of taiga, there are often wetlands—acidic wetlands called bogs, and muskegs, which are wetlands with trees. In these mossy spots, it can be hard to walk on the lumpy, spongy ground. In some bogs, called quaking bogs, the ground underfoot may shake, as if you've stepped on a waterbed or trampoline. That's because there may really be water underfoot: hidden ponds and parts of rivers that have been covered up by peat. Peat is a buildup of moss and other plants that have died. Because moss is acidic, the wetland water becomes acidic, thus preserving the moss in much the same way as vinegar preserves pickles in a jar. These acidic conditions also preserve other things of interest to scientists: ancient pollen and the bodies of woolly mammoths. In 1950, several men in Denmark were digging in a bog when they accidentally dug up the well-preserved body of a man who had died two thousand years before. His skin and leather hat were still intact!

In summer, in northern Finland, even after midnight, you can see well enough to play golf or to shoot some hoops outdoors. Like other places close to the poles, the days are very long in Finland during summer. (This is in contrast to places near the equator, where days and nights are of nearly equal length, all year long.) This effect is caused by the tilt of the earth as it revolves around the sun. In Finland, in summer, the sun may set late at night and stay hidden for only a few minutes or hours. Even after sunset, light from the hidden sun still illuminates the sky and the land. Residents of St. Petersburg, Russia, celebrate these "white nights" of June when light from the sun, hidden under the horizon, bathes the city in an eerie, silvery glow.

The "payback" for long summer days comes during winter. Then, in northern regions, nights are long—very long. The sun hardly rises for several days. Fortunately, during some of the dark times, the northern lights are visible. The northern lights, also called the aurora borealis, light up the sky with splashes of bright red, white, and green that can last for several minutes. These colors are caused by charged particles emitted by the sun that interact with the earth's atmosphere.

TEMPERATE DECIDUOUS FOREST: WHERE BIG LEAVES FALL

South of the taiga, temperatures are warmer, rainfall is greater, soils are richer, and the ground doesn't stay frozen all year. So in these areas, outside cities such as Hamburg, Germany, there's another kind of forest: temperate deciduous.

The temperate deciduous forest stretches from Ireland and eastern France, all the way into Russia. (It's broken up, here and there, by mountains, which have unique climates and biomes, influenced by high altitudes.) The temperate deciduous forest is called temperate because it grows in the temperate, not tropical, regions of the earth. The forest is deciduous because many of the trees are deciduous, meaning they shed their leaves in fall. But before they drop, leaves also turn beautiful colors—yellow, red, gold, and orange. Oak, beech, and chestnut trees are common in these European forests.

INSECTS AND INSECT EATERS

From beetles to bears, temperate deciduous forests are rich in animal life. Woodpeckers, mice, squirrels, jays, rabbits, wolves, foxes, pine martens, polecats, voles, and owls live in temperate forests, too. In Poland there's even a forest-dwelling European bison, a huge, shaggy, twig-eating animal closely related to the American bison of North America's prairies.

*Both polecats (left) and voles (right) find ample food
supplies in Europe's temperate deciduous forest.*

GRASSLANDS: GREAT FOR GRAZING

Like the prairies of North America, the steppes of the former Soviet Union are magnificent grasslands. Tall grasses ripple like ocean waves; wildflowers bloom brightly in spring and early summer. Ribbons of forest grow along deep river valleys that twine between gentle, grass-covered hills. Saiga antelope, wild horses, squirrel-like marmots, wolves, eagles, hares, and small rodents live on the wide expanses.

South of the temperate deciduous forest, in eastern Europe, is a region of steppe. A large patch covers the Great Hungarian plain, which rests in the curve of the Carpathian Mountains. (Budapest, the capital of Hungary, is located here.) On the eastern side of the mountains, the grassland begins again, stretching eastward through the Ukraine and into Russia. The northern part of this area gets enough rainfall for trees to grow. But fires, grazing animals, and farmers who cut back timber keep the trees from growing up,

THE WORLD'S MOST EXPENSIVE FUNGUS

How do you find the world's most expensive fungus, the white truffle? Go for a walk in a forest and take a specially trained pig or dog with you. Their sense of smell will help you sniff out a patch of truffles, which grow underground, among the roots of oak trees in European forests. These mushroomlike fungi are so rare and delicious that they can cost as much as $1,000 per pound! So truffle hunters—people who hunt truffles to make a living—keep the location of wild patches secret. Truffles can be farmed, but because the process can be chancy and difficult, the wild ones are still in demand. Watch what you buy—a few sneaky truffle dealers have been known to switch less valuable fungi for the genuine article or to stuff truffles with small pebbles so the dealers make more money!

Pigs can be trained to detect truffles growing underground.

so it remains grassland. Only a few small patches of forest remain. Farther south, the grassland is dry enough so that trees do not grow well at all.

THE MEDITERRANEAN BIOME

True to its name, Europe's Mediterranean biome is found on the borders of the Mediterranean Sea. It stretches from Portugal—through Spain, southern France, Italy, the Balkan Peninsula, Greece—all the way to Istanbul, Turkey. Although this region gave the biome its name, the Mediterranean biome also occurs elsewhere—in coastal California, Chile, South Africa, and Australia.

If you lived in Athens, Greece, or elsewhere in the Mediterranean biome, you could expect hot, dry summers and cool, wet winters. Low shrubs and groups of evergreen trees are the major plants. Many Mediterranean plants have stiff, hard leaves that are waxy or hairy, which help reduce water loss in dry summers. Common trees include

HEDGEHOGS AND THEIR HEDGEROW HOMES

When a hedgehog is born, it is not prickly at all. Its spines are hidden and flat underneath its skin. But in a few hours, its spines pop through its skin, and days later, they harden, making a hedgehog as prickly as a porcupine. When threatened, a hedgehog will roll up to protect its soft, spineless belly.

European hedgehogs live in Great Britain, western Europe south to Italy and Greece, and parts of Scandinavia and Russia. They're at home in forests and in grazing lands with hedgerows—the brushy areas between meadows. There, hedgehogs dine on beetles, caterpillars, earthworms, centipedes, slugs, and birds' eggs. Many British people even put bowls of dog food out in their yards at night, in case a hungry hedgehog happens by!

In Great Britain, where very little forest remains, hedgerows are an important hedgehog habitat. Hedgerows are living fences—tangles of blackthorn, honeysuckle, bramble, hawthorn, maple, oak, and ash. For centuries, farmers have planted these hedgerows to mark the borders of fields and to keep cows in meadows and away from crops. In hedgerows, wildflowers bloom, butterflies feed, birds nest, foxes hide, and hedgehogs live among the bushes, vines, and trees. Hedgerows are highways for wildlife, which skirt along their edges, and the last refuge for many animals and plants. Unfortunately, these days, some landowners remove hedgerows and install wire fences, so modern tractors and machinery will have more room to work. People concerned about wildlife are encouraging farmers to keep hedgerows, instead of relying on wood and metal fences.

pines and evergreen oaks. Wheat, olives, grapes, figs, and carob grow well in the Mediterranean biome. This region also has oak trees whose bark, called cork, is harvested and used for bottle stoppers, shoes, flooring, and bulletin boards.

SCRUB LAND SCENERY

Forests cover some of the Mediterranean biome. But on much of the land, poor soil, fires, the cutting of timber, and overgrazing by domestic animals keeps forests from growing in. Instead, there are vast areas of scrub—low growing trees and shrubs, including dense thickets of plants.

EUROPE TODAY

The biomes mentioned in this chapter are what naturally exist on European lands. But many of these natural biomes have been drastically changed by people's activities. Great

HERE COMES THE STORK

If it's the month of April, and you live in Europe, and you hear a noise up on your chimney…it could be a stork. In spring, these 3-foot- (1-meter-) tall birds arrive on European roofs, not to bring human babies (as the myths describe), but to build nests and raise chicks of their own. For centuries, white storks have been building massive nests on European chimneys, roofs, haystacks, and church towers. Stork pairs mate for life, and year after year they return to the same nesting site. People generally welcome their presence, considering the beautiful birds to be a sign of good luck.

Europe shares its storks and more than two hundred other bird species with the continents of Africa and Asia. These shared birds, called Eurasian migrants, make amazing twice-yearly journeys of as much as 10,000 miles (16,000 kilometers). Each year more than five billion birds fly south to Africa, returning in spring to breed in Europe. Ducks, shorebirds, hawks, pigeons, and even tiny swifts and swallows make these incredible journeys. In quiet places, you can hear the birds calling high in the air, as they travel at night.

With wingspans of 5 feet 5 inches (1.65 meters), white storks are among the largest migrating birds. The storks' journeys, like so many other aspects of animals' lives, are strongly influenced by weather, natural landscapes, and even the locations of cities. White storks migrate over land as long as they can to avoid traveling over water. So, some head down into Spain, flying the short distance across the Strait of Gibraltar into Africa (Morocco). Others skirt along the Balkan Peninsula, down through Israel, and south to Africa (Egypt).

Like vultures, storks travel by soaring, gliding on warm air currents called thermals. Each day, as air warms and rises, storks spiral up and up into the sky. Because cities are full of concrete, they heat up quickly, creating thermals; so, sometimes during migration, hundreds of storks can be seen spiraling over cities such as Istanbul, Turkey. Storks may pause there before they cross the Sea of Marmara.

Storks' survival is intertwined with people's activities. In the last half century, stork populations have declined drastically. House designs have changed, and not as many structures have the large chimneys storks need for nesting sites. Deforestation has also caused a decline, since storks use trees as nest sites. In addition, pesticides used by farmers to kill insects have decreased the numbers of insects, tadpoles, frogs, fish, lizards, and worms available for the storks to eat. To help storks, people have begun putting up some stork poles, with platforms for nesting sites. European efforts to encourage organic farming—farming without pesticides and other chemicals—could also help these birds. If all goes well, Europeans will be enjoying the spring arrival of the white storks for many centuries to come.

Two European white storks hover over their young.
These storks build large nests on trees, chimneys, and roofs
in Europe. They winter in Africa and southern Asia.

Britain, for instance, was once mostly forested, but the majority of its trees were cut down by settlers long ago. Most of Europe's wetlands have been drained and filled for farms. Large expanses of some of Europe's biomes, such as tundra and taiga, still remain. But others, such as natural grasslands, only linger as small remnants in a patchwork of cities, fields, and farms.

This tree, damaged by acid rain, was photographed in the Bavarian region of Germany. As more and more trees die, increasing amounts of soil wash off the land and into rivers and streams.

SIX

POLLUTION: EAST AND WEST

In the late 1800s, Johann Strauss the Younger wrote a famous waltz called *The Blue Danube.* Unfortunately, these days, Europe's river Danube is more brown, sudsy, and polluted than blue. The Danube, which is Europe's second longest river, starts out in the Black Forest of southwestern Germany, as two clear mountain streams. But then it gets dumped on—or in—all along its 1,800-mile (2,900-kilometer) route.

Fertilizers and pesticides from German and Austrian farms flow into the Danube's waters. Soil washes off treeless German hillsides and into the river because trees killed by air pollution no longer hold the soil in place. In Slovakia, two rivers polluted by 1,700 industries pour chemical filth into the Danube's channel. Farther downstream, sewage and industrial pollution from Hungary, Yugoslavia, Romania, and Bulgaria flow in. By the time it enters the Black Sea, the Danube is a smelly, dangerous mess.

Although the Danube is terribly polluted, it may be on the way to a cleaner future because Europeans deeply care about this famous river's fate. In 1990, 80,000 people stood, arm-in-arm, along the Danube's banks. They made a human chain from Austria to Hungary, demonstrating support for a new park designed to protect the Danube's banks and surrounding areas. This is just one of the many ways Europeans are facing up to their environmental problems and working to find solutions.

EASTERN EUROPE: REVOLUTION REVEALS POLLUTION

For much of the twentieth century, there have been two distinct Europes: eastern Europe and western Europe. Eastern Europe was made up of the Soviet Union and nearby communist countries such as Poland, Romania, Hungary, Bulgaria, and Czechoslovakia. Western Europe was all the noncommunist countries, such as Great Britain, France, Sweden, and West Germany, among others. For decades, neither eastern Europeans nor western Europeans had much contact with one another because the flow of goods, information, and people between eastern Europe and western Europe was restricted by both communist and noncommunist governments.

Then, in the years 1989 to 1991, people in the Soviet Union and eastern Europe overthrew their Communist governments. New countries were formed, almost overnight. Czechoslovakia, for instance, broke into the Czech Republic and Slovakia. The European part of the Soviet Union split into many small countries: Estonia, Latvia, Lithuania, Ukraine, Moldova, Belarus, and Russia. Yugoslavia broke up into Slovenia, Croatia, Bosnia-Herzogovina, Yugoslavia, and Macedonia. East Germans and West Germans rejoiced as they tore down the Berlin Wall. Many families were reunited as these two countries became one Germany again.

THE EAST REVEALED

After these revolutions, for the first time in decades, western Europeans got a peek at what lay behind eastern Europe's borders. What they rediscovered was the warm and wonderful people of eastern Europe. But what they also found, in many areas, was terrible pollution. In places, the snow was black from falling through polluted air. Some lakes and rivers were unsafe for swimming or fishing, and the water was undrinkable because of human sewage and chemicals flowing from industrial plants. Poland's Vistula River was so polluted that most of its water couldn't even be used in factories because it would ruin the machinery! These tragic environmental situations continue today in parts of the former Soviet Union and eastern European countries.

ENVIRONMENTAL ILLNESSES

Many eastern Europeans suffer from pollution-related conditions such as lung disease, irritated eyes, skin diseases, high cancer rates, and high rates of birth defects. One third of the people who live in Magnitogorsk, Russia, have asthma, chronic bronchitis, or other diseases that make it difficult to breathe. The local steel mill—the world's largest—pumps out plumes of black smoke that blanket the city. Elsewhere in Russia, in Kiev and Moscow, medical mysteries—sudden baldness among hundreds of children, widespread skin diseases, neighborhoods where an unusually high number of children were born without left forearms—may be linked to severe pollution, but money for studies and treatment of the problems is scarce. In Russia, more than half of all schoolchildren are in poor health. Life expectancy—how long a person is expected to live—has dropped by two years in the last few decades. In contrast, in other European countries, life expectancies have been on the increase, partly because of breakthroughs in medical technology.

Smokestacks fill the air over Magnitogorsk, Russia, with soot, endangering the health of the people who live nearby.

LOOKING AT CAUSES

Why do eastern European countries, including the Republics of the former Soviet Union, suffer from such pollution problems? One reason is that much of eastern Europe's economy depends on heavy industries, factories that manufacture chemicals, steel, and heavy machinery, and produce a lot of pollution. Most eastern European factories are old and use out-of-date equipment, which has very few pollution controls. What makes conditions worse is that eastern Europe burns a lot of brown, lignite coal for energy. This kind of coal, when burned, produces more pollution than the hard coal used elsewhere in Europe.

NOT FREE TO SPEAK

Another factor in the environmental decline of eastern Europe has been politics. For decades, the Soviet Union and governments in eastern Europe did not give their citizens the right to speak out and protest. So the environmental activism that helped create better laws and pollution controls in western Europe lagged behind in eastern Europe. Environmental activists in communist countries had to risk their jobs, and sometimes their lives, to spread the word about environmental problems. Nevertheless, in the 1980s, people did eventually protest about environmental problems such as the pollution of the Danube.

My Friend Rita

Behind every environmental event, no matter on what continent or in what country, are individual people. One is my friend Rita. She's a refugee from Moldova, a new republic that is located north of the Black Sea, in eastern Europe. Every week, I tutor Rita in English. And she teaches me about Europe and Russia and much more. When she left Moldova a few years ago, she could hear gunfire from her home. Her country was in a civil war. Guns and tanks on one side of the river targeted those on the other side, blasting both shores. So Rita, her husband, and her two children fled to the United States and started a whole new life.

Rita is happy and grateful to be in America. But it is a hard life for her. She left her job as an engineer in Moldova. Now she must learn a new language, go to school, and work as a waitress to survive.

Rita and I often talk about the pollution in eastern Europe. She reminds me it is not polluted everywhere. She came from a place where there wasn't much heavy industry. The air and water were quite clean. In fact, she finds the air and water in our Indiana town much more polluted than in Moldova.

Our air sometimes stinks from the ethanol factory, and the tap water turns muddy after heavy rains and tastes bad. Rita is surprised, because she had heard that America did not have any pollution at all!

Rita is also shocked by the amount of junk mail and paper that Americans throw away. Paper was expensive in her home, so it was not wasted. "Don't people know forests are cut down to make paper?" she asks. We often share our environmental concerns. Rita says, "I think everybody in all countries must cooperate to reduce pollution because, like we say in Russia, 'Zem lya nash obshii dom,' or 'The earth is our global house.'"

FUTURE PLANS

Today the countries of eastern Europe, including the former Soviet Republics, are beginning to tackle their environmental problems. But they have little money for pollution cleanup. Fortunately some other nations are helping out, sending experts and investing money to help eastern Europe switch to industrial equipment that pollutes less. Local environmentalists also are working hard. For example, Ecolion, a group in former East Germany, planted thousands of trees and is pushing for pollution controls. Poland is working with other European countries as part of the European Ecological Network, which sets aside and protects natural areas. These efforts are positive steps toward an environmental cleanup, a cleanup that promises to be a challenge because these countries must at the same time undergo radical changes in their economic and political systems.

WESTERN EUROPE

Compared to people in the rest of the world, most western Europeans are wealthy. Fifteen of the world's twenty richest countries are in Europe. Switzerland is at the top. Western Europeans live industrialized lives, with telephones, televisions, cars, and good health care. Food and drinkable water are available to most. Western Europeans also live a long time, and very few of their infants die, which indicates the general quality of their lives is good.

Despite these advantages, western Europe still faces environmental problems. Plastic pollution fouls beaches. Oil tankers wreck, spilling thousands of tons of oil that kills fish and birds. Smog shrouds some cities in a brownish haze that makes it difficult for many people to breathe. Ironically, much of the pollution is a by-product of the automobiles, manufacturing, and the fossil fuels, such as coal, oil, and gas, needed to run all the equipment that is part of an industrialized, "modern" lifestyle.

The countries of western Europe, however, are making great strides in safeguarding the environment. They have worked hard to develop new technologies that create less pollution than the old equipment did. One of the countries that has reversed its attitude toward environmental issues is Germany.

GERMANY'S TURNAROUND

In the early 1980s, West Germany's government wasn't very pro-environment. It resisted many ecologically inclined actions, such as banning spray cans that used chemicals that destroy the earth's ozone layer. Germany's national goal seemed to be economic prosperity, despite the environmental price. But then, in the late 1980s, Chancellor Helmut Kohl helped lead Germany in a new direction. Germans began seeing environmental issues not as problems but as opportunities. They figured, if the world was going to need technology to reduce pollution, then Germany would develop, build, and sell it! Soon, the government and private companies began putting money and energy into new, more environmentally sound technologies.

GREEN GROUPS

Of course, it wasn't just a desire to make money that pushed Germany's environmental turnaround. Its environmental problems were becoming impossible to ignore. Forests in Germany were dying from acid rain. In 1986, radioactive pollution from the explosion of the Chernobyl nuclear plant (in what was then the Soviet Union) blew into Germany and threatened to contaminate crops there. Because of concern about environmental problems, more and more people joined Die Grünen, the Green Party, which had been started in 1980. Die Grünen was the world's first political party to focus pri-

THE CASE OF THE PEPPERED MOTH

You probably already know that air pollution can kill trees and make people cough. But did you know that it can change the course of evolution? The proof lies in the color of the peppered moths of England.

At one time, almost all the peppered moths in Great Britain were white with tiny dots and spots of black. (These black spots, which look like pepper, were the inspiration for this moth's name.) Only a very few, individual peppered moths were black.

But then, things changed. In the 1800s, during the Industrial Revolution, British factories and homes started burning a lot of coal. Thick, black smoke spewed out of chimneys and smokestacks, darkening the skies, the buildings, even the bark of the trees. Things changed for the moths, too.

By 1900, only one tenth of the moths near Manchester, an industrial town, were white with black spots. The rest—most of the moths—were black. It's not that the moths suddenly turned color, like chameleons. Scientists suspect birds, which eat moths, played a role in the change.

White peppered moths had once been hard to see against the white, lichen-covered tree bark. But pollution killed the lichens and colored the tree trunks gray. Against the darkened trees, the white moths were easy to see. The birds gobbled them up! The few black moths, however, were hard to see against the dark background. So fewer of them were eaten by birds. As the years passed, more and more of the black moths survived and went on to lay eggs. The eggs, naturally, would produce mostly black moths. Over time, the lighter colored moths died off and the black ones survived. The peppered moth had evolved. This darkening, because of pollution, is called industrial melanism. It has affected not just peppered moths but other moths, plus ladybugs, spiders, and even pigeons in some areas.

marily on ecological issues. The Greens gained support and managed to get members elected to political posts in Germany. Green parties also sprang up in Austria, Belgium, Finland, and other countries. The popularity of these parties has decreased since the 1980s. But they have had a big impact on politics. In many nations, other, more powerful, political parties have begun including environmental change in their set of goals for the future.

MORE EUROPEAN EFFORTS TO PROTECT THE ENVIRONMENT

In recent years, western Europeans have been among the world's leaders in developing better environmental laws, technologies, and habits. They have spearheaded efforts to

Today, scientists are witnessing a turnaround in some parts of Great Britain. In places, more and more of the peppered moths are lighter in color today. Environmental laws have helped reduce pollution, especially the black particles in coal smoke. And instead of burning coal, people are burning oil. As a result, the lichens are growing back. Tree bark is growing back in its natural, unstained lighter color. So more of the white moths are surviving. In one scientist's garden, the percentage of black moths has decreased from 93 percent in 1959 to 33 percent in 1990!

A white peppered moth (left) is clearly visible, and vulnerable, on the bark of a dark tree. The black moth (right) can barely be seen.

pass international treaties to protect the environment. In the late 1980s, international agreements were made to protect Antarctica, the oceans, and the ozone layer. The European Union, an organization of fifteen countries that coordinates economic issues, now has a special department working on environmental issues, continentwide.

Individual European countries are also making environmental progress. For instance, Denmark has installed high-tech water treatment plants, excellent pollution controls, and turbines that generate electricity from wind. The Danish government has imposed higher taxes on oil, gas, and coal. This extra expense has encouraged people and companies to be more energy efficient. From 1979 to 1989, the country decreased its energy use by 22 percent!

Meanwhile, Sweden has decreased its release of sulfur dioxide—a major air

A recycling plant in the Netherlands turns toxic plastics (PVCs) into ladies' handbags. The increased environmental awareness of the people of Europe is evident in programs such as this one.

pollutant—by 80 percent in the last twenty years. Great Britain has cleaned up the Thames River, which was smelly and filthy; and fish populations have started to rebound. The Netherlands is saving energy and material by recycling 62 percent of its paper and cardboard and 31 percent of its aluminum. These and hundreds of other European environmental programs are showing terrific results.

ENVIRONMENTAL PROBLEMS ON THE HORIZON

Acid rain and water pollution aren't the only environmental concerns Europe faces. Other environmental problems are likely to cause trouble in the future.

BOMBS AWAY: THE NUCLEAR THREAT

For decades, the Soviet Union built up its supply of nuclear weapons, preparing to defend itself. But now that the Soviet Union has broken into smaller, independent countries, these dangerous weapons are scattered among numerous new, struggling nations that aren't equipped to handle them. In some cases, there may not even be enough money to heat the silos where the missiles are held! Mishandling these missiles could cause environmental disaster on a global scale.

Europe is also a major consumer of nuclear energy. Disposing of radioactive waste from nuclear power plants and nuclear submarines could be a problem in the future, as well.

A Sinking Feeling: Wetlands Loss

Wetlands are home to many plants and animals and are breeding grounds for many commercially important fish and shellfish. Wetlands also filter out pollutants from water flowing through them. Yet even as far back as 1703, people destroyed wetlands. Czar Peter the Great built the city of St. Petersburg, Russia, on marshes in the Gulf of Finland, so he'd have access to the Baltic Sea and western Europe. Today, as space gets more and more scarce in Europe, and the continent gets more crowded, there's increasing pressure to destroy the few remaining wetlands, in order to build homes, farms, and other developments. In addition, peat bogs, a type of wetland, are mined to extract peat, which is burned for fuel in countries such as Ireland.

Forests Under Pressure: Deforestation

Much of the southern European forest has already been cut and cleared for agricultural land. Increasing demand for paper and wood products could endanger the taiga, which is still mostly intact.

A Whale of a Problem: Arctic Pollution

Fourteen nuclear reactors and thousands of barrels of toxic waste lie in Arctic waters, in the Barents Sea and the Kara Sea. Years ago, Soviet submarines deposited the waste there, with no special safeguards. Arctic fish, whales, seals, and other animals are endangered by the toxic and radioactive materials—but the Russians do not have the money to clean them up.

Soil Loss and Farming Trouble

Russia is blessed with a region of chernozem—thick, black fertile soil where plants grow well. But improper farming methods churn up the soil, allowing it to blow away and run off into rivers. Twenty-five percent of this soil has already been lost. Soil loss is a problem elsewhere in Europe, too.

Turning Up the Heat: Global Climate Change

Most scientists worldwide agree that the earth's climate is warming overall, because air pollution is increasing the amounts of "greenhouse gases"—water vapor, carbon dioxide, methane, nitrous oxide, and chlorofluorocarbons—in the atmosphere. These gases, like the glass walls of a greenhouse, trap heat in the earth's atmosphere. The predicted effects of global warming include melting of the polar ice caps, flooding of low-lying coastal areas, and shifting weather patterns. Europe, which has many low-lying coastal

One of the world's worst environmental disasters, the explosion at the Chernobyl nuclear power station, occurred near Pripyat, Russia. On April 26, 1986, a reactor exploded, causing its core to melt down and release radioactive material. Exposure to radioactive material can be extremely dangerous, causing radiation sickness. Nausea, vomiting, and diarrhea, and in the long term, cancer, may be the result.

Geography played a role in the spread of the radiation. Winds blew Chernobyl's plume of radioactivity far beyond the Soviet Union's borders. Radioactive particles rained down onto Poland, Finland, Sweden, and Norway. In affected areas, people tried to avoid the risks of radiation by throwing away the vegetables from their fields and not drinking milk or eating meat from cows.

Soon afterward, the Soviet government evacuated 134,000 residents that lived within 20 miles (32 kilometers) of the plant. They erected a huge building to store the remains of the reactor that exploded. But almost 5,000 nuclear plant workers continue to live in the area, monitoring the old reactor and running the plant's other two reactors, which still generate power. Following the breakup of the Soviet Union, the Ukraine is now saddled with this immense disaster area. There's no way to clean it up entirely. Nuclear experts from western countries say the two reactors still running are unsafe, and the building that contains the melted reactor is leaky and unstable. But Ukraine is short on money and needs electricity from the plant. So western nations have donated money to help Ukraine shut down the reactors by the year 2000.

Several hundred people died in the first months after the Chernobyl disaster. But the effects of the explosion are still being felt today. People who lived in the area, or who

areas such as the Netherlands, could be very vulnerable to these changes. Temperature and weather changes could devastate crops, forests, and wildlife.

EUROPE: A PLACE OF CONFLICT AND COOPERATION

In Europe, a single river may flow through many different countries, as the once-blue Danube does. Air pollution from a factory blows past guard towers, fences, and gates. Moose, butterflies, and fish take no notice of national boundaries as they walk, run, fly, and swim on natural routes they've followed for thousands of years.

People, however, do see these borders. Europe is a crowded continent of many small countries, many nationalities, many languages, and many cultures. This variety is the worked on the cleanup, have an increased risk of cancer, birth defects, and miscarriages. Some workers suffer from a syndrome dubbed "Chernobyl AIDS" because, like AIDS, it damages the immune system. Childhood thyroid cancer is on the rise. Many cancers take a long time to develop, however, so the full effect of the nuclear accident may not be known for years.

An abandoned playground is surrounded by empty apartment buildings months after the disaster at the Chernobyl Nuclear Power Plant.

spice of life on the continent. But over the years these differences have also caused bloody conflicts, such as the recent civil war in Bosnia.

Today, Europe is a good example of both conflict and cooperation. In places, wars and political disputes among countries keep some European nations from tackling environmental problems together. But elsewhere, many countries who were traditionally enemies are cooperating to safeguard wildlife and clean up rivers, lakes, and the air. For instance, many European countries have "sister" parks—parks on each side of a border they share with another country. The two countries often work together to manage the plants, animals, and resources in both parks. All in all, Europeans are making great strides toward a worthy goal: a peaceful, clean, prosperous Europe, which all of them can share.

GLOSSARY

acid rain   general term for precipitation that has been acidified by pollution in the air

altitude   vertical elevation above sea level

biome   an area that has a certain kind of climate and a certain kind of community of animals and plants

chernozem   dark, rich layer of fertile soil found in grassland

circumpolar   circling one or both of the earth's poles

climate   a region's long-term weather conditions

conifer   a tree that bears cones, such as pine cones

continent   one of the seven great masses of land on Earth

deciduous   plants that drop all their leaves each year

equator   the imaginary line that runs around the earth's middle

Eurasian migrant   a bird that lives part of the year in Europe or Asia but also makes a long journey to travel elsewhere in Europe or Asia, or even to Africa

fjord   a narrow inlet of sea between cliffs or steep slopes

glacier   a large mass of slow-moving ice

humidity   the amount of water vapor in the air at a certain temperature, as compared to the maximum amount of water vapor the air can hold at that temperature

hydroelectric   having to do with the generation of electricity by water power, usually by dams that capture the energy of flowing, falling water

industrial melanism   animals' evolution of darker fur, feathers, or shells in response to environmental conditions created by soot and other dark pollutants produced by industry

latitude   a measure of distance, north or south, relative to the earth's equator

Pangaea   the original landmass (or supercontinent) that existed two hundred fifty million years ago, when the separate continents we know today were all joined together

Panthalassa   the ocean that surrounded Pangaea

peninsula   a piece of land that is nearly surrounded by water but is still connected to the mainland

permafrost   permanently frozen ground

plain   a large area of flat or gently rolling countryside

plateau   a large piece of land that is raised above the surrounding area and is relatively flat-topped, like a table

sea   a subdivision of the ocean; seas are lobes of ocean partly surrounded by land

sea level   the level of the surface of the sea, midway between high and low tide

stalactite   an iciclelike structure, made of calcium carbonate, that hangs from the ceiling of a cave

stalagmite   a calcium carbonate structure, like an inverted stalactite, that points upward from the floor of a cave

supercontinent   a gigantic continent (Pangaea) that existed long ago, which later broke up to form the smaller continents we know today

tectonic plate   a large piece of the earth's crust that slides over molten rock below, gradually shifting its position on the earth's surface

thermal   a rising mass of warm air

ARCTIC OCEAN

Arctic Circle

ASIA

Reykjavik ○ ICELAND

NORWEGIAN SEA

FINLAND

SWEDEN

NORWAY

Helsinki ○

Oslo ○   Stockholm ○   Tallinn ○   RUSSIA

ESTONIA

NORTH SEA

Riga ○

GREAT BRITAIN   DENMARK   LATVIA

Dublin ○   LITHUANIA

IRELAND   Copenhagen ○   Vilnius ○

Amsterdam ○   Minsk ○   Moscow ○

London ○   NETH.   Berlin ○   Warsaw ○

Brussels ○   GERMANY   BELARUS

BELGIUM   Luxembourg ○   Prague ○   Kiev ○   KAZAKHSTAN

Paris ○   LUX.   CZECH REP.   UKRAINE

ATLANTIC   SLOVAKIA

OCEAN   Bern ○   LIECH.   Vienna ○   Bratislava ○

SWITZ. ○   Vaduz ○   AUSTRIA   MOLDAVIA

FRANCE   Budapest ○   Chişinău ○

Ljubljana ○   Zagreb ○   HUNGARY

Andorra   MONACO   SLOVENIA   CROATIA   ROMANIA

la Vella ○   BOSNIA-   Belgrade ○   Bucharest ○

Monaco ○   SAN MARINO   HERZEGOVINA   BLACK SEA

ANDORRA   San Marino ○   Sarajevo ○   YUGO.   BULGARIA   GEORGIA

PORTUGAL   Madrid ○   Corsica   ITALY   Sofia ○   Tbilisi ○   Baku ○

VATICAN   Rome ○   Tiranë ○   Skopje ○   MACEDONIA   AZERBAIJAN

SPAIN   CITY   ALBANIA   TURKEY

Lisbon ○   Sardinia   GREECE   AEGEAN SEA

Sicily   Athens ○

MALTA ○

Valletta ○   Crete

Political Map
of Europe

○ Capital

0 _____ 400 miles

0 _____ 600 kilometers

MEDITERRANEAN SEA

AFRICA

INDEPENDENT COUNTRIES LOCATED IN EUROPE

NAME	CAPITAL
Albania	Tiranë
Andorra	Andorra la Vella
Austria	Vienna
Belarus	Minsk
Belgium	Brussels
Bosnia-Herzegovina	Sarajevo
Bulgaria	Sofia
Croatia	Zagreb
Czech Republic	Prague
Denmark	Copenhagen
Estonia	Tallinn
Finland	Helsinki
France	Paris
Germany	Berlin
Greece	Athens
Hungary	Budapest
Iceland	Reykjavik
Ireland	Dublin
Italy	Rome
Latvia	Riga
Liechtenstein	Vaduz
Lithuania	Vilnius
Luxembourg	Luxembourg
Macedonia	Skopje
Malta	Valleta
Moldova	Chisinău
Monaco	Monaco
Netherlands	Amsterdam
Norway	Oslo
Poland	Warsaw
Portugal	Lisbon
Romania	Bucharest
San Marino	San Marino

INDEPENDENT COUNTRIES LOCATED IN EUROPE *(Continued)*

NAME	CAPITAL
Slovakia	Bratislava
Slovenia	Ljubljana
Spain	Madrid
Sweden	Stockholm
Switzerland	Bern
Ukraine	Kiev
United Kingdom	London
Vatican City	———
Yugoslavia	Belgrade

INDEPENDENT COUNTRIES LOCATED PARTLY IN EUROPE, PARTLY IN ASIA

NAME	CAPITAL
Azerbaijan	Baku
Georgia	Tbilisi
Kazakhstan	Almaty
Russia	Moscow
Turkey	Ankara

FURTHER READING

(Material geared for young readers is marked with an asterisk.)

* Agel, Jerome. *Where on Earth: A Refreshing View of Geography*. New York: Prentice Hall Press, 1991.

Bevan, Nicholas. *Atlas of the New Europe*. New York: Henry Holt, 1992.

Bryson, Bill. "Linking Europe's Waterways," *National Geographic*, August 1992, 3–31.

Crawford, Peter. *The Living Isles: A Natural History of Britain and Ireland*. London: British Broadcasting Corporation, 1985.

Daly, Douglas C. "The Leaf That Launched a Thousand Ships," (The Potato Famine), *Natural History*, January 1996, 23–35.

* Dickinson, Mary B. *National Geographic Picture Atlas of Our World*. Washington, D.C.: National Geographic Society, 1993.

Edwards, Mike. "Lethal Legacy: Pollution in the Former U.S.S.R," *National Geographic*, August 1994, 70–98.

———. "Living With the Monster: Chernobyl," *National Geographic*, August 1994, 104–115.

* Green, David R., editor. *The Eyewitness Atlas of the World*. London: Dorling Kindersley, 1994.

Hammond, Allen, editor. *The 1992 Information Please Environmental Almanac*. Boston: Houghton Mifflin, 1991.

* McCuen, Gary E., and Ronald P. Swanson, *Toxic Nightmare: Ecocide in the USSR & Eastern Europe*. Hudson, Wisconsin: Gary E. McCuen Publications, 1993.

National Geographic Editors. "The New Europe," (a map), *National Geographic*, December 1992 insert.

Parker, Sybil P., editor. *World Geographical Encyclopedia, Volume 4: Europe*. New York: McGraw-Hill, 1994.

* Rosenthal, Paul. *Where on Earth: A Geografunny Guide to the Globe*. New York: Knopf, 1992.

Schwartz, David M. "Hurray For Hedgehogs!" *International Wildlife*, March/April 1990, 22–26.

Strain, Priscilla and Frederick Engle. *Looking At Earth*. Atlanta: Turner Publishing, 1992.

* van Rose, Susanna. *The Earth Atlas*. London: Dorling Kindersley, 1994.

* Wood, Robert W. *Science for Kids: 39 Easy Geography Activities*. Blueridge Summit, PA: TAB Books, 1992.

INDEX

Page numbers in *boldface italics* refer to illustrations.

1- 7/02
3- 6/04